MEMORY OF A KISS

poems and situations

John Curl

MEMORY OF A KISS

poems and situations

Photos by Robin Roth

Cover: Frederick Stuart Church, *Circe*, 1910.

ISBN: 978-1-7335775-1-9

Homeward Press
Berkeley, CA
https://johncurl.net/

MEMORY OF A KISS

Memory of a Kiss
Call of the Wild
All's Fair in War and Love
Must I Atone For Roses?
Thanks for Reminding Me
Nothing in the End
I Used to Think I Was a House
Love and Learn
The Guide Told Me
Sunrise on the Dark Side
That Perfume of Understanding
Invisibility
Following Your Nose
Do Unto Others
Tropical Butterfly
Palette Knives
Dreaming Possible Dreams
Old People
So This Is How It Feels
A Little Knowledge
Hiking on Sinai
Descent into Darkness
Listening
Scentimental
The Ultimate Secret

He who kisses joy as it flies by
will live in eternity's sunrise.
— William Blake

MEMORY OF A KISS
poems and situations

MEMORY OF A KISS

Back when my hair
was wild and I was
doing donuts
trying to figure out
who I was,
my eyes ruled
my heart. But
vision is a fickle lover
in the pastures
of imagination,
or so I learned
more than once
the hard way.
So at that point
I was longing for
something different,
some special connection,
and if it wasn't special,
I'd rather be alone.

I remember the exact
instant that
all changed, when
the broken pile of
dry leaves and dead twigs
I kept locked and hidden
in my core suddenly
started to move and glow

as our lips touched
for what felt like
somewhere between
infinity and eternity.

Alone with you here,
the curve of your neck,
the grace of your hands,
the melodies and harmonies
in your voice,
the incantations woven into
the fringe of your shawl,
the subtle scents and auras
that surround you,
your secret smiles
have me enraptured.
I feel suddenly like
we have shared this space
countless times before,
in other eras,
other bodies.
Lie with me here tonight
on this cloud,
fly with me,
summon your genie, Circe,
rub your spirit lamp for me.
I am shipwrecked
on this desert isle,
rescue me, drape your hair
across my imagination,

wrap me in feelings,
weave your entranced fabric
of shooting stars around me,
enmesh me in your carpet,
let the mother of creativity
fill your tongue with spells,
sortilege and enchantments,
and our eyes with emotions,
braid endless webs
of song around
our shared and shattered dreams,
lift me, my magic bird,
with your slight of hand,
escape with me
over the waves,
let me dangle
from your bracelet
like a charm, Circe,
I am your toy,
let me hang from
your claws as we fly.

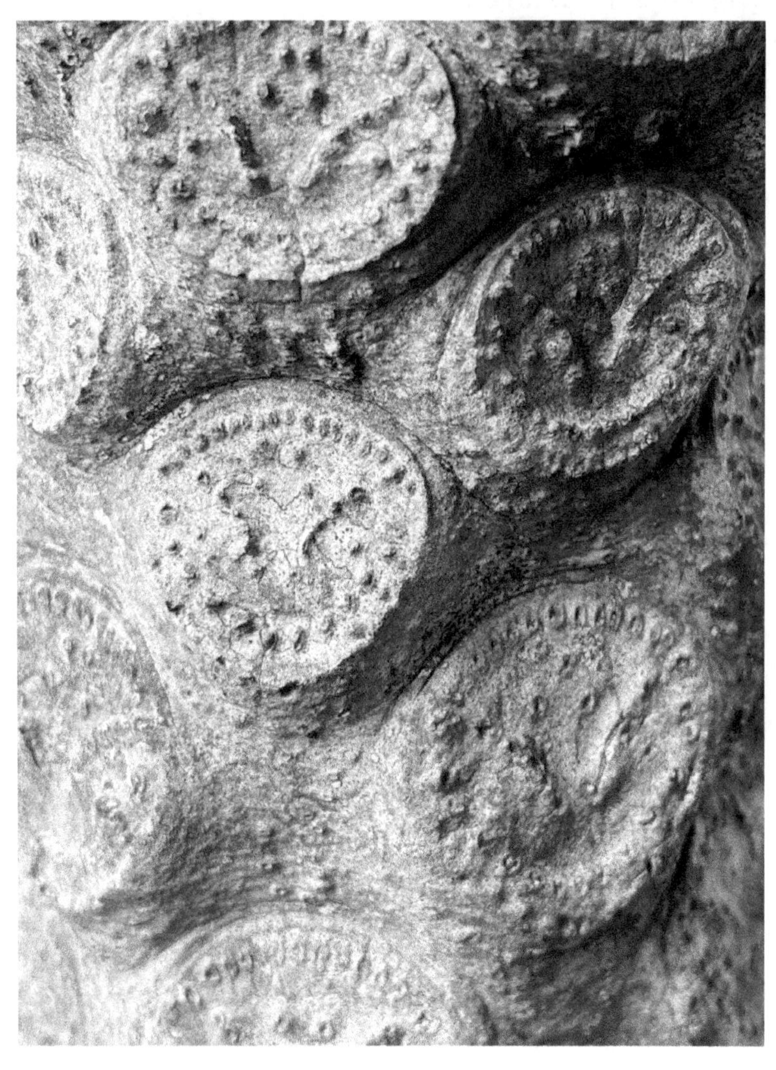

Photo by Robin Roth

CALL OF THE WILD

I knew we still had some unfinished
business, though I didn't know
what it was, some drama or comedy
or tragedy to play out.
It wasn't a good thing or a bad.
I knew it had nothing to do
with good or bad.
I can't explain it in any reasonable
way, because it also had
nothing to do with reason.

I flew halfway around the world to get
away from you, but the farther I flew,
the stronger something pulled me back.

I grew up in the inner city, where I
learned to trust my instincts by
navigating the dark streets and alleys.

I knew you would be trouble
from the get-go, but I was out
looking for trouble. It was
all my fault. I admit it. I was a
deck of cards looking to be played.
There you have it.
That's the whole story.
I was clueless.
I got dealt a lot more

than I bargained for, and I didn't
even realize I was bargaining.

One minute we were relaxing on a raft
on a lazy river, and the next minute
we were whirling down the rapids.
I was playing hearts, but I got it
back from you in spades.

Maybe we were under some
potion or spell.
Or maybe we had some
karmic debt to work out.

Tonight I'll just call it the call of the wild.

A million Monarch butterflies return to
southern Mexico every autumn
after migrating thousands of miles
to Canada, but no individual butterfly
completes the round trip. The ones
who return are the great grandchildren
of the Monarchs who left Mexico
five months earlier. Four generations
are born and die over the course
of their annual migration, yet
they somehow never lose
the way back to their destination.

Tonight I'll just call it the call of the wild.

ALL'S FAIR IN WAR AND LOVE

I built her on the crystal sands,
out of fragments of dreams,
garbled lyrics, unheard songs
and wind melodies, but
daddy warned me what's in store
when you challenge those above
and mama taught me long ago
all's fair in war and love.

I followed her at midnight down
a meandering woodland stream,
and promised to exchange my stars
for a taste of her moonbeams, but
daddy warned me what's in store
when you challenge those above
and mama taught me long ago
all's fair in war and love.

She beckoned me to follow her
through a dense canebrake,
beside the water's edge,
just before daybreak,
we sat upon a marble rock,
my heart began to ache,
I gazed into her misted eyes
and made my worst mistake.

The rattles knotted in her hair

made a frightening sound,
she offered me her hand,
petals floated to the ground.

A butterfly alighted on a
spray of Queen Anne's lace,
she handed me an artist's brush
and said to paint her face.

She shook her wavy locks,
out tumbled seeds and bones,
she walked into the marble rock
and left me there alone, but
daddy warned me what's in store
when you challenge those above
and mama taught me long ago
all's fair in war and love.

MUST I ATONE FOR ROSES?

Must I atone for roses?
For their intoxicating fragrances?
For the exquisite petals I love to touch?
For bleeding on their thorns?
Must I suffer for roses
because I've enjoyed them?
Or because we have destroyed them?
Is this my reward or our curse?
They wilt and fall
into a petal-shrouded hearse.

Late at night behind the servants' entrance
to the magic castle, the apprentices gather
to test their skills on the cheap,
the boys playing card and hat tricks,
the girls playing for keeps.

You got to be able to distinguish
good spells from bad, if you want
to practice sorcery. You learn
to know up by knowing down.
You can't fake enchantment.
When it's there, it's there.
First we yearn to lose our innocence
then we mourn our loss.

Leave your demons playing
sleight of hand with each other

around the dark corner.
What does the past matter?
I give you my breath, then
you give it back to me. This
moment here with you is
breathtaking. Isn’t that enough?

The brief time we spend together
in this garden
with these roses feels
stolen from eternity.
Weep with me here,
mourn, and heal.
Weeping is atonement
enough. Embrace
this all too short
time we share.
Come with me now,
and steal these roses
from eternity.

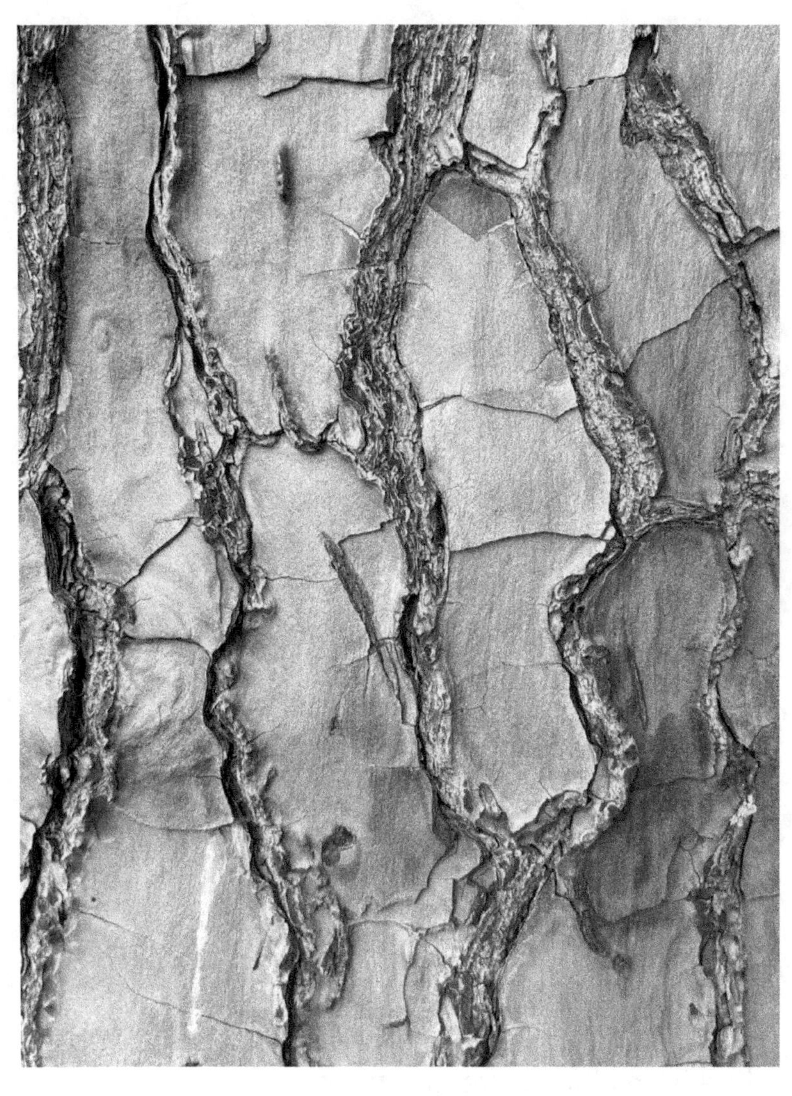

Photo by Robin Roth

THANKS FOR REMINDING ME.

Before my core ever melted for
the very first time, before I ever
fully lost my stillborn heart in
this sandstone desert heat, I
worried if I was capable of
whatever I imagined love to be.
She comes only in her own good
time, or she doesn't come at all.
Two planets spinning in orbit
around each other.
Intimate others.
I had heard so much about
what intimacy is and isn't.
Then I devoured love, swallowed
it in such huge gulps that only
left me drowning in limestone
caverns and thirsting
at the same time.

She sighed into her pillow. "Do
we have to?" "No," I replied,
"We don't have to." And
at that instant for the first
time in my life I gave up on sex.

For the longest time after that
I had no interest in love. There
was no one I wanted to join my body

with. I didn't want to get involved.

Ever since I'd come of age, I'd
either been with a partner or been
looking for one. Without a partner
I'd felt ungrounded, without a center.
Now some tectonic plate had shifted
inside, and I wanted only to be alone,
I wasn't looking for a partner, I didn't
want to be in a couple. For the first
time in my adult life, I was happy
to be alone, single. I no longer felt the
need for an intimate other.

Am I still capable of feeling?
Of touching someone? Or letting
someone touch me? Or
am I so remote now that
no one dares come near?

Then you reminded me.

Long before we were
women and men, long
before we were straight and
gay and everything else,
long before we were human,
according to ancient
Aristophanes and Plato,
the Creator designed us

not as female and male,
not as two but as
one whole creature,
all-inclusive, double-gendered,
bi-sexed.
Yet we did not appreciate
our self-sufficient wholeness
but became arrogant
and presumptuous
so in punishment the Creator
split us in half, cut us each
into two, creating the sexes, the
genders, and ever since, we're been
lonely, longing, searching
for our other half, thirsting for
the intimacy of rejoining with
our other self, and becoming
whole again.

The last time I felt this way was
in a different lifetime. Just touching
someone like this, so casually
intimate. I'd forgotten
how it feels to merge submerge
into some shared space some place
that is neither you nor me, but both
of us, familiar, comfortable in a special
way, cozy yet vast as the universe.

NOTHING IN THE END

From the crowd of endless eyes,
to the mists of eternity,
dispelling all your
hopes and fears,
as if from nowhere,
the eyes of the one
you've been waiting for
suddenly appear,
my friend, but then again,
it all comes to nothing in the end.

To feel your skin against mine,
flesh to flesh.
Is there anything more
intimately wonderful?
That sweet warm space
our bodies share
when essence joins
our common core
into this special place that is
both of us,
and we remember once again
that this is
how all the world should be, but isn't,
my friend, but then again,
it all comes to nothing in the end.

But the way love grows,

whenever I'm near you,
drenched in wild desire
to exist inside you
the way you exist inside me,
the moment is everything,
worth more than the world,
and then it's gone,
all except our memories
and our longings
and the endless repercussions
of our loving acts,
but then again,
love is all that lives on
and gives meaning to this world,
my friend,
it all comes to loving in the end,
it all comes to loving in the end.

I USED TO THINK I WAS A HOUSE

When you were a rumpled blouse
and I was a torn tee shirt,
before you were somebody's spouse
and I was dumber than dirt,
I thought I was a house
along a winding country road.
I had a foundation
I had a roof
I had plumbing
I was wired
I had furniture
I had rooms
I had a washer
I had a dryer.

When I was a wild jack
in your hand of marked cards,
when I mistook you
for a comet
soaring through my stars,
when I rode the melodies
taunting your guitar,
when I wandered
through your spice closets
lost in your bazaar...
You had ceilings
you had floors
you had stairs

you had walls
you had a basement
you had halls
you had windows
you had doors.

When you were a rumpled blouse
and I was a torn tee shirt,
before you were somebody's spouse
and I was dumber than dirt,
I thought I was a house
along a winding country road,
I thought I was your home
and you were my abode.

LOVE AND LEARN

Thinking with your heart,
getting in touch with your heart,
trusting your heart.
It didn't come easy to me.
Did it always come easy for you?

I loved my family and pets of course,
but of course
romantic love was different.

Learning to think with your heart.
Learning how.
How to get in touch with your heart,
how to trust your heart.
And learning when.
Learning when to think with your heart,
when to get in touch with your heart,
when to trust your heart.

And when not.

Love and learn.

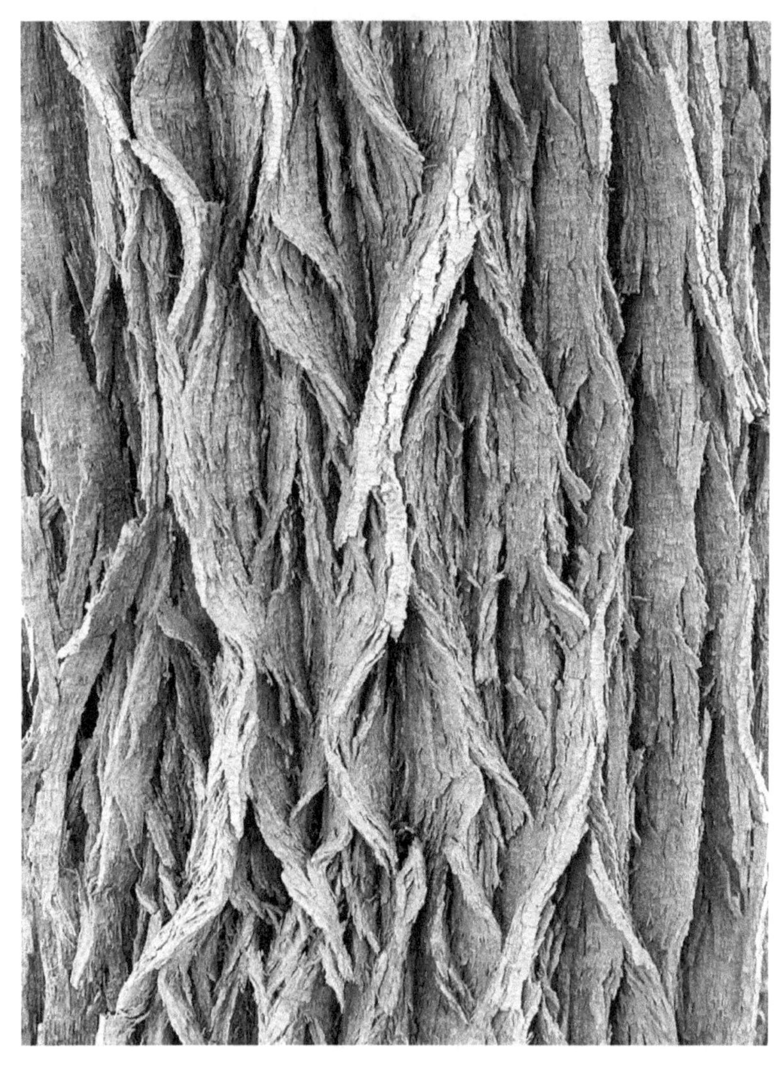

Photo by Robin Roth

THE GUIDE TOLD ME

I watched you grow and change
those many years. The love
we shared, that you gave
me and I gave you,
the pains we shared, that you
caused me and I caused you,
the innumerable ecstasies and
dreams, disappointments, betrayals,
unnecessary and necessary, sweet
souvenirs, old photos and
painful scars we left each other,
mostly faded now but never
to totally fade away.

How could you have done all
that to me? How could I have
done all that to you?

The guide told me we each have
many bodies and identities, beyond
comprehension by ourselves,
much less by any other person.
And now that it's over, finally
over, your eyelashes still so long
and crisp, when your mind and spirit
and all your energetic and etheric
bodies slipped out of your shell
and joined the universal life,

I kissed, peacefully, so peacefully.
I kissed one last time your forehead,
one last time even now
I kiss you goodbye.

Open the window.
Close the window.

SUNRISE ON THE DARK SIDE

In the human psyche,
the moon has always been
attached to our emotions
and both the moon and
our emotions have forever
had a light side and a dark.

The moon's dark side
—the far side—
has always been shrouded in
intimations of the mysteries,
dangers, temptations
of the unknowable.

Until photos came back
showing that the dark side
of the moon is really
just as light
as the near side.

Lost in blind alleys
of the labyrinth,
they keep killing each other
again and again,
lies dripping acid
over the piles of
ruined lives and burned roofs,
although we're all just

travelers through this dark
side of the earth,
no one except
grifters and executioners
leading the way before us
or stalking us from behind,
our options all played out
our meager gains all reversed
no dreams left in our back pockets,
no longer expecting succor
from the best
or pity from the worst,
while all around us
wild creatures and aspen forests
flee toward the sheer cliffs,
wondering whether or not
it's worth it to stay alive
or just succumb and go extinct.

Yet when your spirit
suddenly brushed mine,
my balance was reversed,
and when you touched my hand,
all secrets were revealed,
and when we spoke,
clouds dispersed,
and when your lips
brushed my cheek,
I understood what it was all worth,
and when you struck my

bones like a tuning fork,
all the everyday lies
meant nothing in the universe,
and when you whispered
incantations in my ear,
I heard only
the innermost meanings
of rebirth,
and through
all the toxic smoke and shadows,
through all the lost blind alleys
of the labyrinth,
It was suddenly
sunrise
on the dark side of the earth.

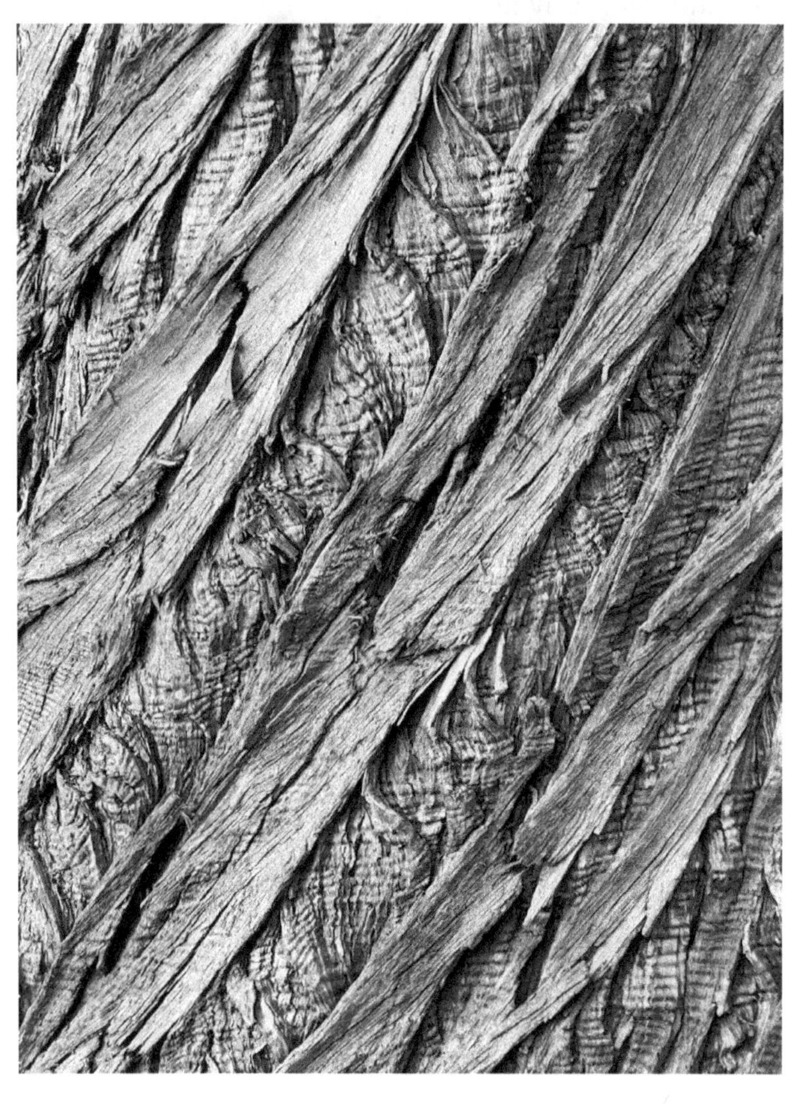

Photo by Robin Roth

THAT PERFUME OF UNDERSTANDING

That low musical tone,
that cosmic note,
droning but thrilling,
always in the background,
behind or below or above
the noise and chatter
of daily life,
punctuated by
everyday wails and moans,
broken and bitter
screams and explosions.

That seemingly empty space
between contradictory thoughts,
between conflicting realities,
between loves and enemies,
between broken hearts.

Can you hear it?
Can you smell it?
Can you touch it?
Can you feel it?

It's there all the time,
inside the stench of
wounded creatures.

You can hear it when you

breathe with your heart,
you can smell it when you
listen with your soul,
you can feel it when you
sense with your spirit,
you can touch it when you
reach out with your intentions.

Those lighting flashes
through the forest,
that living energy
everywhere around us,
that source of all inspiration,
all renewal,
that future surging forth
from the ruins of
everyday lost time.

That perfume of understanding.

INVISIBILITY

Everybody said how great kindergarten was. That's where all the big kids were. At first it was kind of fun. Sometimes I even liked learning stuff. First and second grades were OK too.

Mostly I just put up with it. I kept waiting for it to get better, but third grade only got worse.

The worst part was the regimentation. I understood that taking orders in school was preparing me for the grownup world, but from what I knew of that, I wanted no part of it. In movies I'd seen how they break horses. I was a wild colt and they were trying to break me.

As I sat in class, increasingly alienated, my resistance stiffened; then I hit a wall. Something inside snapped. I decided to escape, to make my getaway.

Instead of going to school one morning, I slipped away to the park and hung out all day with the birds and squirrels. I knew my parents would be mad, of course, so I didn't mention it to them. I did that for a few days, until the truant officer caught me.

Under the bright lights of the principal's office, with my parents there, I realized that I was in an existential crisis, and decided that my best survival strategy was invisibility. I decided to lay low and play along with them for now. I made myself into a small transparent bug on the wall.

From that vantage point, I passed a number of my formative years, watching human society with endless curiosity and a certain amount of contempt, at the same time as I was participating in my life.

I almost even forgot that I had once not been invisible. Until one day it hit me that my normal state was feeling confined.

Suddenly I didn't want to live at all if I had to live like that.

I stretched my elbows and realized I was inside something, a container, a bubble, a sack, an invisible cocoon.

I spread my arms and lifted them, and to my surprise, the bubble burst. I saw that my arms were really wings. I lifted them and began to speak my mind.

FOLLOWING YOUR NOSE

"Just follow your nose,"
was mom's advice.

Of course, I always had it
with me, so I couldn't
forget and leave
home without it.
And my nose
was always out in front,
leading me when
I wasn't running sideways
or hopping backwards.

What Mom meant, of course,
was to trust my instincts.
Her advice usually
worked pretty well,
while I was little.

In our neighborhood
were both brightly-lit
avenues and shadowy alleys,
streets where sweet fragrances
wafted and called
like nectar to hummingbirds,
from florists, bakeries,
and restaurants.

And there were also

back streets reeking
of garbage and urine.

Mom's advice
worked pretty well until
I grew big enough
to begin following
sweet scents
into dark alleys.

These too
beckoned to me,
with the attractions
of the unknown,
of adventure,
perilous flames calling
to spiraling moths.

DO UNTO OTHERS

When you wound a hummingbird,
when you slash a maple tree
when you crush a wilted daffodil,
when you trample a honey bee,
when you poison children's minds
to prevent them from seeing
the world as it is
and as it was meant to be,
when all crimes against humanity
drain blood from the least of these,
their blood rains down on you and me.

Here in this grownup world
of corporate nations and endless wars,
when you try to hide the truth
with cunning words and lies,
when you accuse your victims
of your own war crimes,
when you say it all just means
I will murder you
or you will murder me,
you think I do not see,
but when you maim the innocents
you mutilate you and me.

Do unto others
mama taught you and me.
Do unto others

crying on her knee.
Do unto others
the playground creed,
lesson learned easily or
cruelly received,
spit into the wind,
find out what it means.
Do unto others
while our grandchildren plead.
Do unto others
while our cities bleed.

TROPICAL BUTTERFLY

Here we are once again,
emerging from another chrysalis
at the end of another spiral
of life or death or life, surrounded
by crimes so vast that they
convict the entire system.
That's why they're afraid
to put him on trial.

But must we do
what we must do,
whatever it takes,
wherever it takes us?
We are all artists and artisans
inside this painting.
Human civilization guilty
as charged.
Our only hope is
calm in the center of chaos,
surrounding ourselves in
the acceptance of death
and life and love,
in the timetable
of transformation.

A tropical butterfly
lands on the only flower
left standing and with exquisite

sadness slowly opens and closes
her brilliant turquoise wings
over and over again.

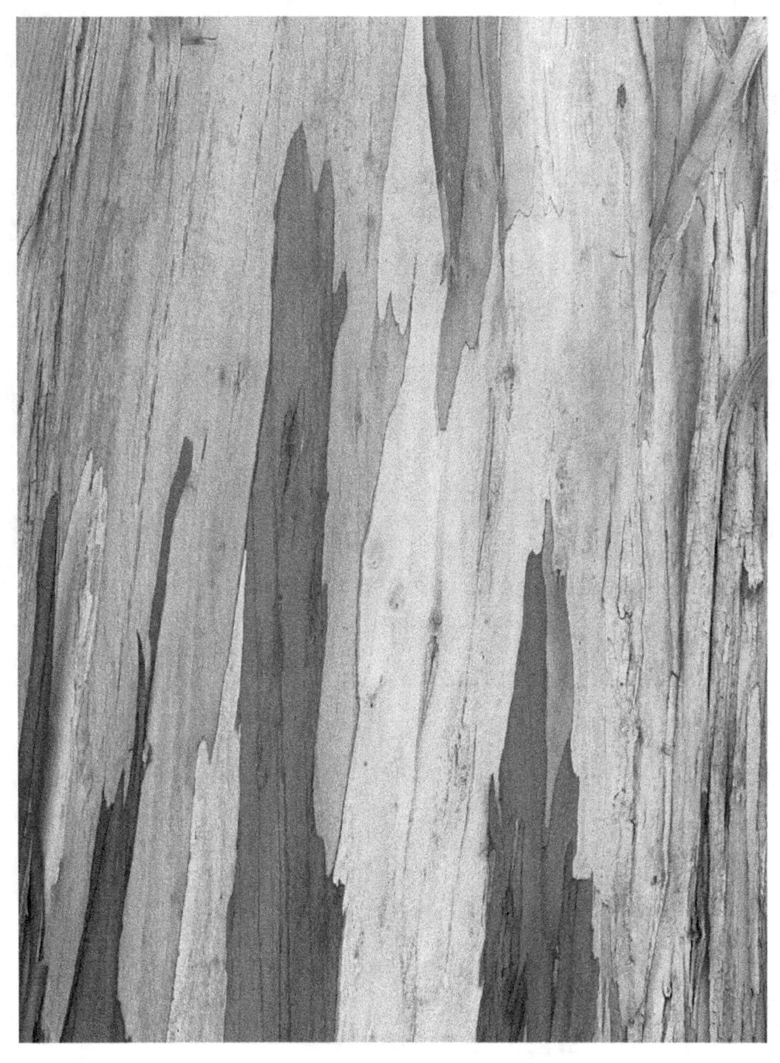

Photo by Robin Roth

PALETTE KNIVES

"An artist can never remove
anything from a canvas, you can
only add to it; even
when you take a palette knife
and scrape off the paint, you
are still adding to it." That's what
an old artist friend
of mine said a long time ago.

We can't erase mistakes.
Our lives are like that.
We might
wish we had done things differently,
apologize or try to make
restitution for wrongs
we've done to others,
words thoughtlessly spoken,
accidents that didn't have to happen,
but we cannot
withdraw them. Just as we can never
erase the great crimes
and injustices of history,
war, conquest, slavery, make them
to have never happened.
Our past words and acts can never be
undone, no matter how much
we might wish to. We can never remove
the past. What happened, happened.

Words once spoken, acts once acted,
are forever.

We exist only in this moment,
with our memories of the past,
which may or may not be accurate,
and our
dreams of the future.
A hand appears and writes on the wall.

DREAMING POSSIBLE DREAMS

Impossible dreams are wonderful
but even more wonderful
are possible dreams.

Remember when you cast away
some foolish delusions, abandoned
some childish fancies,
discarded some deceptive dreams?
But when you cast away
those impossible illusions,
did you also cast away
your possible dreams?

Lying in bed one night,
to my amazement
I felt very light, I was floating
above the covers, and by just thinking it,
by willing it, and slightly shifting
my shoulders and hips left or right,
I could rise and fall,
move about the room
wherever I wanted to go.
I soared through the window,
above the roof tops, into the sky.

Then I woke. Today
I still wonder as I
lie sleepless on my pillow,

is gravity holding me back,
or my own disbelief?

I too was once a future dreamer,
musing about
the world as I wished it to be.
But everything is what it is,
and everything is also what it seems,
a story's not over when it ends,
daybreak doesn't always come at dawn,
a life's not gone until its songs fade away,
waking isn't the cessation of dreams.

Nothing is ever what it should,
paradise is never nearer,
but when the perfect
becomes enemy to the good,
it should be understood
that the reflection is standing
in front of the mirror.

Insisting on impossible dreams
makes possible dreams impossible.

Dream possible dreams.
Revolution is the art of the possible.

OLD PEOPLE

Now that I'm older I
understand more about
our deep drive to somehow
reverse time,
even just for an instant,
to feel once more
the emotions we might
never feel again,
to glimpse once more
our lost youth.

When I was small—obviously
I hadn't thought it through—
I had the notion that old people
had always been old,
just like a pigeon had always
been a pigeon or a cat a cat.

Mom used to take me out
shopping with her, and
on certain street corners
she would meet other
neighborhood women who
every day gathered to chat.
Some of them seemed
around Mom's age,
but others looked really aged
and fragile, with blue veins and hair.
When an occasional old man

stopped and said hello,
the older women twittered.
They talked on and on
about medical problems,
which somehow seemed
endlessly interesting to them.
I was constantly squirming
to drag Mom away.

I didn’t actually know many old
people well, beyond my grandpa,
who lived with us. He told me
about things he’d done when
he was my age, but I still
never thought of him as young.

Today people see me
as an elder too,
but when I look at you
and touch your hand,
I don't see four thousand weeks or
feel the weight of thirty thousand days.

I see a girl, a boy, a beautiful toddler.

Let the purring cat sit on your lap
scratch her behind her ears,
Play peek-a-boo with baby.

Old people aren’t old.

SO THIS IS HOW IT FEELS

Despite or because
in the larger picture
we are them and they are us.

In a time of
mass murder and genocide.

Back in the old days
of daily print newspapers,
if you didn't like the headlines,
you could always turn
to the comics.

Almost out of butter.
Where did I put my keys?
Home team lost or won.
Celebrities filed for divorce.
The advice columnists
are scandalized.
Coffee cup needs washing.
Bananas turning brown.
Late fees in the account.
Nails need trimming.
Keep walking in circles.
Past the expiration date.
Mailbox stuffed with junk again.
Everyday life goes on while
the everyday abuses all around us

keep spiraling ever downward
in slow motion at all times
into the bottomless abyss.
We can't go on like this.
Yet we do.
We've got to do something.
Immediately.
Yet we don't.
We must change now
or face the consequences.
No one else is going to do it.
But who am I?
But what? But how?

After every hopeless disaster,
our world somehow
finds a way
to pick ourselves up and
to start over again.

So this is how it feels
to go about daily life
in 21st century America.

A LITTLE KNOWLEDGE

Is it too late? Will we never lay to rest
this harsh justice? Are we forever
outcasts sentenced here
to repeat this purgation
for eternity? How can we get past
those righteous swords of flaming
retribution without destroying us all?

In the middle of the garden were
two trees, the tree of life and the tree
of the knowledge of good and evil.

God said, "You must not eat
the fruit from the tree
of the knowledge of good and evil
or you will die,"

"You will certainly not die," the serpent
said. "But if you eat that fruit,
your eyes will be opened, and
you will become Godlike,
knowing good and evil."

Thus America's founders lost
whatever original innocence
they might have had
when they committed
our country's Original Sins,

and covered their shameful
transgressions with lies.

And thus and so we
the living generation inherited
the consequences of those
crimes against our sisters and brothers,
against ourselves, against humanity,
against life itself, and to this day,
so it is written, we bear that
crushing weight, and even now
at the Garden gate a flaming sword
flashes back and forth, blocking our way.

In this perilous journey together
to our common fate, how can we find
our way back together to the Tree of Life?

As they say, a little knowledge
can be dangerous.

HIKING ON SINAI

My head exploding with grief,
I tore myself away
from the everyday misery
that my people inflict on each other,
the incessant explosions and screams,
and I went hiking through
the foothills of Mt Sinai, where,
between the jagged rocks
and crumbling sand dunes,
I stumbled on two men
in Bedouin garb
at a camp fire.

They muttered, "Ya Marhaba,"
and strangely, to my own surprise,
"Ya Marhabtayn," I replied,
as if I knew their tongue.

We drank jiggers of sweet black tea
and fed the flames with camel dung
and laughed until
the thin moon set in the pale west,
then I wrapped myself in my thoab,
my head sank slowly
into my pillow of sand,
and I surrendered to the sounds
of the mountain desert shadows:
the chatter of rosefinches;

the cries of red-tailed hawks;
the whispers in the breeze,
floating sacred melodies across the sky
through the long Mt Sinai night,
ancient visionary songs that
sounded almost like the voices
of the prophets themselves,
as if it was Mohammed himself
singing the Call to Prayer, the Adhan,
and at the exact same time,
Moses himself singing
the Kol Nidre, the All Vows
on Yom Kippur, the Day of Atonement.
Oh, those deepest assonances,
those harmonious dissonances.
Am I the only one who hears them?
Am I the only one who hears
Moshe singing the Kol Nidre
while al-Amin sings the Adhan,
together, above the roar
of exploding buildings and children's screams?
Am I the only one who hears
the operatic duet of the tragic Prophets?

DESCENT INTO DARKNESS

This morning
I watched sunrise
through my bedroom window
and saw the world descend
once more into darkness.

Unfolding
before our eyes:
above the rubble
of what was once a
fabled metropolis,
through the toxic smoke,
the warlords of chaos,
destruction and death
descend
once again triumphant.
Behold!

Why do our people
choose to
destroy ourselves
over and over
and over again?

Some fracture
in our DNA perhaps,
or some curse?

This cycle of tribe violence,
grievance and revenge
against ourselves:
the innocents become the victims,
the avengers become
the oppressed,
the oppressors transform
into innocents,
and the cycle
of grievance and
revenge staggers on
and on.

Haven't we already suffered
enough death?

Apparently not.
Our people seem to always
seek out the darkness,
something inside
always seems to ache for
another new bloodletting.

Yet our people also
always emerge at the end,
draped in black shawls
burying and mourning our dead,
shedding unending tears,
and rebuilding our shattered
communities once again.

Will we never somehow
break this curse
or transcend it?

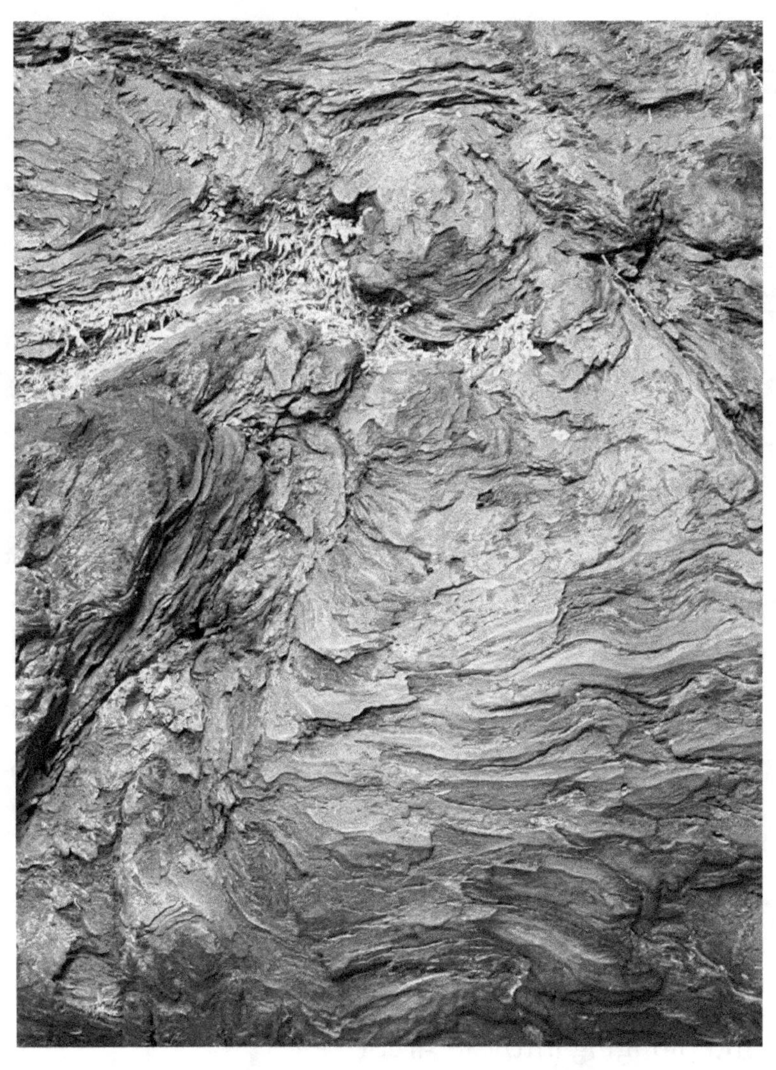

Photo by Robin Roth

LISTENING

Listening is more than hearing.

The chirping
of a flock of small birds.
Waves crashing.
Wind rustling
through willow branches.
Distant music.
A child moaning.
Your lover whispers
sweet nothings in your ear.

Listening is paying attention.
Listening is being attentive,
opening your mind
to what those sounds mean.
Listening can lead
to understanding.

Those waves are crashing
from great ice chunks
breaking off melting glaciers
and plunging into the Arctic sea.
Those chirping chickadees
are warning that an owl is near.
Those moans are
cold and hungry children
sobbing themselves to sleep.

That distant music
is a protest march.
Listen to the hollow sounds
of skulls cracked by billy clubs.
Your lover holds you tight
and whispers
it's going to be alright.

Listen to the sound of water
flowing up from the ground,
through the slow-moving sap
of ancient bristlecone pines.
Listen to the sound of magma
slowly flowing through
the center of the earth.

Listening is more than hearing.
Listening is paying attention.
Listening is being attentive,
opening your mind
to what those sounds mean.

Listen to the chants
rustling in the wind,
listen to the lovers
whispering in the dark.

SCENTIMENTAL

Scentiments
Scent of new mown grass
scent of salty sea air
scent of dry rose petals
scent of a baby's head
scent of simmering pasta sauce
scent of seaweed on a beach
scent of old childhood photographs
scent of ripe tomatoes on the vine
scent of fields of black-eyed susans
scent of oregano and thyme
scent of a spring breeze
scent of an ancient mangrove swamp
scent of a game trail through a pine forest.

Scentiments
scent of an old steamer trunk
scent of a piano in a dive bar
scent of mahogany sawdust
scent of mustard and sauerkraut
scent of a wet hound dog
sent of sweaty socks
scent of rat poison
scent of the fires at an oil refinery
scent of the toilet in a bus station
scent of the monkey house at the zoo
scent of antiseptic in a hospital ward
scent of a subway train in a heat wave
scent of a grandfather climbing
out of a dumpster

scent of a cop at your car window
scent of a heart attack at the amusement park
scent of a politician's bank account
scent of stock brokers breaking into cold sweats
scent of the secret interrogation room lights
scent of a prison cell block at lockdown
scent of nothing in the refrigerator
scent of a burned family album
scent of a candidate's makeup
scent of white lilies alongside caskets
scent of soldiers kicking bodies into trenches
scent of the end of the war
scent of just retribution.

Scentiments
scent of early morning dew on clover
scent of your childhood bedroom
scent of a book that hasn't been
                    opened in a long time
scent of a mind that hasn't been
                    opened in a life time
scent of children's imaginations
scent of mother's milk
scent of the corners of your smile
scent of the back of your neck
scent of your deepest kisses after sex
scent of tears of joy.
Scentiments.
Scentimental.

THE ULTIMATE SECRET

The secret is balance
the secret is what makes it art
the secret is the difference between cormorants,
loons, coots, and grebes
the secret is somewhere inside the mountain
the secret is what you see when you open
                    your eyes in the morning
the secret is the thought you just forgot
the secret is peeling back the onion
the secret is whispering in your ear
the secret is strings of brightly colored beads
the secret is chewed by a polar bear
the secret is a sucker punch
the secret is the holes between the words
the secret is truth and consistency
the secret is deeper inside dark clouds
the secret is the instant before you fall asleep
the secret is the accents and the herbs
the secret is the turquoise of the petals
the secret is touching the energy spots
the secret is remembering your center
                                        of gravity
the secret is understanding your limits
the secret is linking your breath, pace and stride
the secret is riding that music to wherever
                                        it takes you
the secret is respect for the craft
the secret is the discipline of the easy

the secret is where the opposites cross
the secret is all around us at all times
the secret is the password that touches
                    your heart
the secret is the best and the worst are
                    true at the same time
the secret is opening yourself to it
the secret is stretching to just before
                    the breaking point
the secret is we are citizens everywhere
                    in an infinite world
the secret is we are tiny creatures
                    in a microscopic world
the secret is there are no rewards beyond
                    our acts themselves
the secret is in the wrist
the secret is there are always deeper layers
the secret is this poem never began
                    and will never end
the secret is the opposite of what you think it is
the secret is the opposite of what I just said.
The ultimate secret is that there are no secrets.

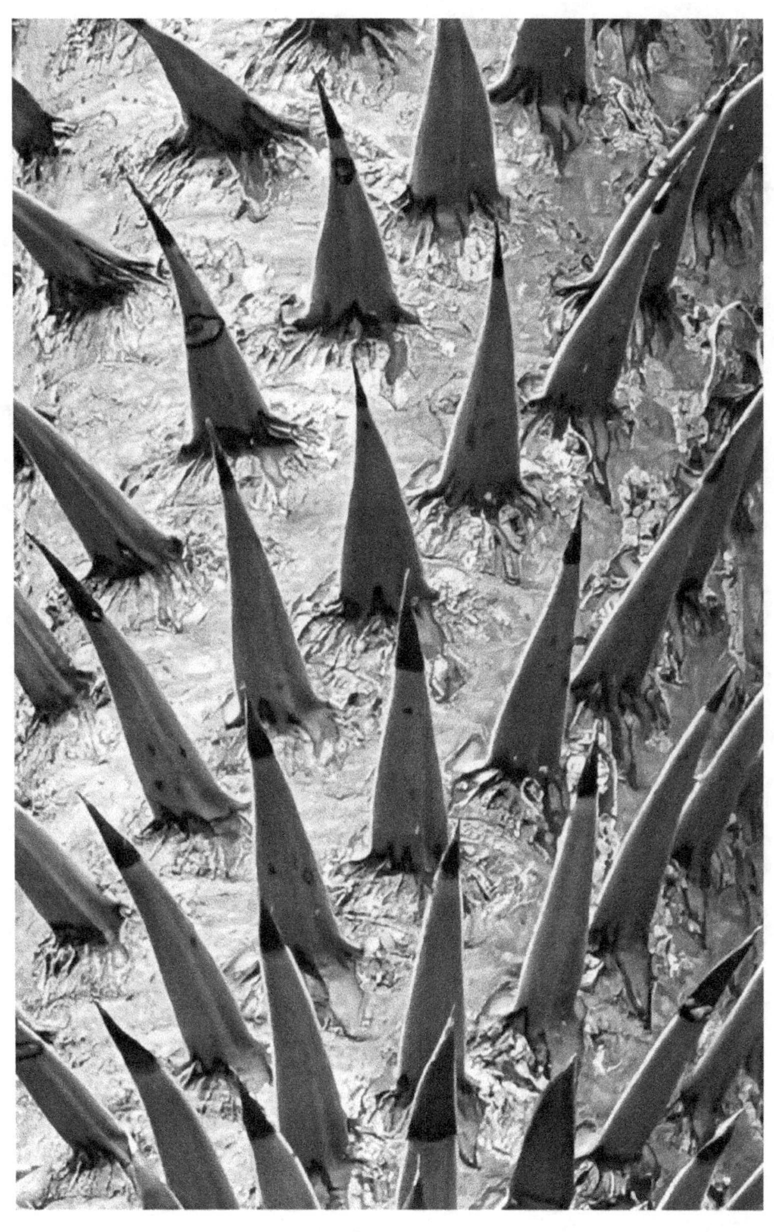

Photo by Robin Roth

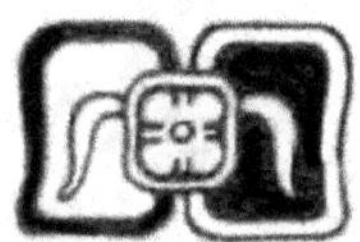

ABOUT THE AUTHOR & PHOTOGRAPHER

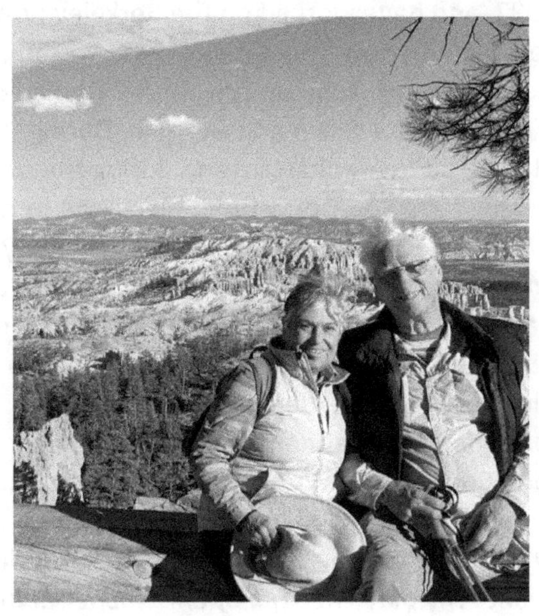

JOHN CURL

I am author of twelve poetry collections, two novels, a memoir, and several histories. My translations of Inca, Maya, and Aztec poets are collected in *Ancient American Poets*. I was one of the founders of Indigenous Peoples Day in 1992, and have worked on the Berkeley powwow since then. Born in New York City in 1940, my family was a mixture of Romanian-Austrian Jew, Irish Catholic, English-Scottish Protestant, French and German. During the winters I grew up in Manhattan, and during the summers in New Jersey farm country without electricity or running water. My father was a post office worker, and my mother had been a dancer in Broadway musicals. I have a degree in Comparative Literature from New York City College, with a semester at the Sorbonne in Paris, France. I reside in Berkeley and have one daughter. I was a professional woodworker and cabinetmaker for over forty years at Heartwood Cooperative Woodshop. I served as chair of West Berkeley Artisans and Industrial Companies, and as a Berkeley planning commissioner. I was vice-president of PEN Oakland. My play *The Trial of Christopher Columbus* was produced by the Writers Theater in 2009. My transliterations from Pachacuti's Quechua formed the libretto for Tania León's *Ancient* (2009). I represented the USA at the World Poetry Festival in 2010 in Caracas, Venezuela. I have been a member of the Revolutionary Poets Brigade of San Francisco for many years, and an editor of their annual anthologies.

website:
https://johncurl.net/

ROBIN ROTH

I love to hike in natural settings, where I am developing my eye for photography. Several iPhone photography classes have been valuable in developing my skills. In vocation, I'm a health educator, health advocate, and health activist. After working as a medical record administrator in hospitals and clinics, I found right livelihood at City College of San Francisco teaching in the Health Education and Women's Studies Departments. There I created the Women's Health Issues class, the HIV/HCV Prevention Educator program, taught Human Sexuality, Harm Reduction, Health & Aging, and related classes. Happily retired after 40 years, I love running into former students all over SF, especially at rallies and demonstrations. I'm also retired from chairing the SF Hepatitis C Task Force, but still active in promoting Single Payer Healthcare for All, women's health and social justice issues.

My photos and a photo essay as well as a poem have been published in Vistas and Byways, SF's Osher Lifelong Learning Institute's online journal. The photos in this book are close-ups of tree bark, part of a longer photo essay. I'm a lifelong learner, taking classes in a variety of subjects, practicing QiGong, TaiChi, and Yoga, gardening, traveling, delighting in my friends and family, biological and intentional, and especially in adventuring with my grandchild.

ALSO BY JOHN CURL

Poetry:
America Beyond the Well (Homeward Press, 2025)
Rainbow Weather (Vagabond Books, 2022)
Yoga Sutras of Fidel Castro (Homeward Press, 2014)
Revolutionary Alchemy (Homeward Press, 2012)
Scorched Birth (Beatitude Press, 2004)
Columbus in the Bay of Pigs (Inkworks /Homeward, 1991)
Decade (Mother's Hen, 1987)
Tidal News (Homeward Press, 1982)
Cosmic Athletics (Poetry For The People, 1980)
Ride the Wind (Poetry For The People, 1979)
Spring Ritual (Cloud House, 1978)
Insurrection/Resurrection (Working People's Artists, 1975)
Commu 1 (Gnosis Press, 1971)
Change/Tears (Drop City, 1967)

Poetry Translation:
Ancient American Poets (Bilingual Press, 2005).

Memoir:
Memories of Drop City (Homeward Press, 2008).

History:
Indigenous Peoples Day (IPD Books, 2017)
For All The People (PM Press, 2009, 2012)
History of Collectivity in the San Francisco Bay Area (Homeward Press, 1982)
History of Work Cooperation in America (Homeward Press, 1980).

Fiction:
The Outlaws of Maroon (Homeward Press, 2019)
The Coop Conspiracy (Homeward Press, 2014)

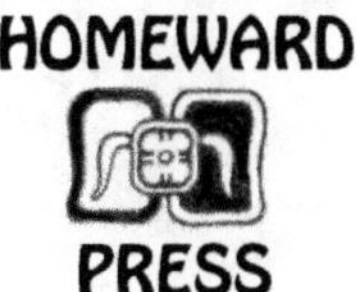
HOMEWARD
PRESS

www.ingramcontent.com/pod-product-compliance
Lightning Source LLC
LaVergne TN
LVHW020656100826
845148LV00012B/2523